MW01628849

I like you just the way you are!

— Angie Hunt

IF I HAD LONG, LONG HAIR

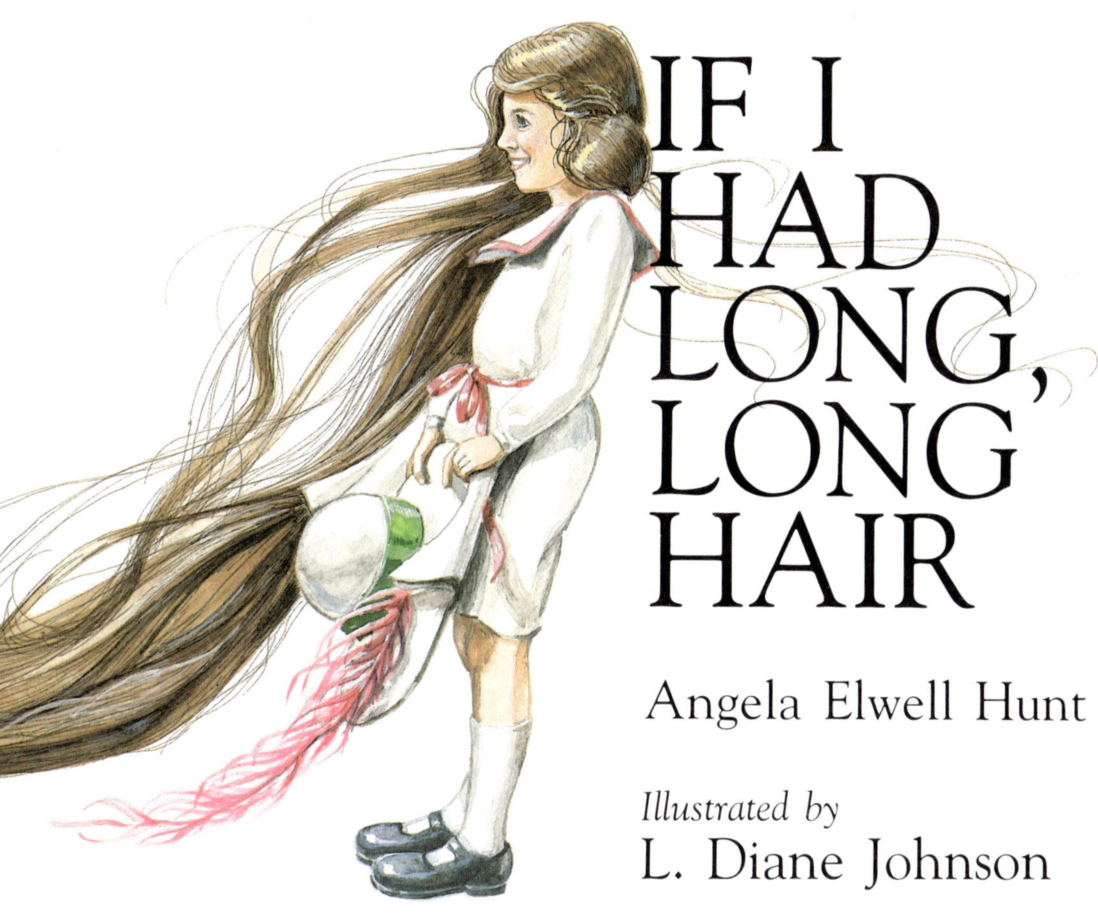

IF I HAD LONG, LONG HAIR

Angela Elwell Hunt

Illustrated by
L. Diane Johnson

ABINGDON PRESS
Nashville

IF I HAD LONG, LONG HAIR

This book is printed on acid-free paper.

Library of Congress Cataloging-in-Publication Data

Hunt, Angela Elwell, 1957-
If I had long, long hair / Angela Elwell Hunt: illustrated by L. Diane Johnson.
p. cm.
Summary: Loretta ponders both the good and bad things that might happen if she had long, long hair, hair long enough to flow around her like royal robes but also long enough for hamsters to nest in.

ISBN 0-687-18683-8 (alk. paper). ISBN 0-687-18684-6 (lb. bdg. alk paper)
[1. Hair—Fiction.] I. Johnson, L. Diane, 1951- ill. II. Title.
PZ7.H9115If 1988
[F] —dc19 87-24140

PRINTED IN HONG KONG

To Taryn Li

A.E.H.

To Dad and Mom

who are young at heart

L.D.J.

My name is Loretta Littlefield, and there is something I want very much. It is not a chocolate candy bar or a bag of spicy potato chips or a coloring book with a box of new sharp crayons. It is not . . . .

. . . a baby doll that talks and
rolls her eyes, or a bed with a
canopy on top for my room.

What I want is something that Daddy can't buy for me and Mother can't make for me. Not even my dog can help me.

I wish I had long, long hair.

If I had long, long hair, I'd put it in two braids and let my friends jump rope with me.

If I had long, long hair, I'd pretend I was Queen Loretta.

Whenever I'd walk down stairs, my hair would cascade behind me like majestic, royal robes.

If I had long, long hair, I'd lie in bed at night with my hair spilling over the foot of the bed.

It would cover the floor and
sparkle in the moonlight.

If I had long, long hair, I'd ride in a parade with my hair streaming behind me. People would say, "There goes Loretta with the long, long hair!"

I'd smile and wave to them.

If I had long, long hair, my mother could sew with my hair instead of thread. I'd give her one hair each day, and that night a new one would grow to replace it.

If I had long, long hair, I wouldn't need clothes. I'd always be covered up.

If I had long, long hair, I could sweep Mother's kitchen all by myself. I'd simply walk across the floor, and my hair would sweep just fine.

But if I had long, long hair, people might step on it. Ouch!

I'd have to wear a sign saying, "Careful! Here comes Loretta with the long, long hair."

And if I had long, long hair, it wouldn't fit into the sink for washing.

I'd have to hang my head out the upstairs window and let my mother hose it down.

If I had long, long hair and tried to pile it on top of my head, I couldn't get through the doorway!

If I wore my long, long hair in braids, my friends might tie me to a tree and leave me there.

If I had long, long hair, it would drag on the sidewalk whenever I went skating in my neighborhood.

As I pulled it down the sidewalk, it would get tangled and messy. Bicycles, dogs, and joggers might run over it.

"Loretta, your long, long hair looks like a rat's nest!" my mother would say.

If I had long, long hair that looked like a rat's nest, maybe mice, squirrels, gerbils, and their friends would come to live in my hair.

I'd be the only kid on my block with hamsters in my hair.

So if I had long, long hair, I'd probably ask my mother for a haircut.

I think I'll be happy just the way I am.